What does it mean to have

Sickle-Cell Anaemia

Louise Spilsbury

Heinemann

C0000 002 034 807

www.heinemann.co.uk/library
Visit our website to find out more information about Heinemann Library books.

To order:
☎ Phone 44 (0) 1865 888066
📄 Send a fax to 44 (0) 1865 314091
💻 Visit the Heinemann Bookshop at www.heinemann.co.uk/library to browse our catalogue and order online.

First published in Great Britain by Heinemann Library,
Halley Court, Jordan Hill, Oxford OX2 8EJ,
a division of Reed Educational and Professional Publishing Ltd.
Heinemann is a registered trademark of Reed Educational and Professional Publishing Ltd.

OXFORD MELBOURNE AUCKLAND
JOHANNESBURG BLANTYRE GABORONE
IBADAN PORTSMOUTH (NH) USA CHICAGO

Designed by AMR
Illustrated by David Woodroffe
Originated by Dot Gradations
Printed by Wing King Tong, Hong Kong.

ISBN 0 431 13923 7 (hardback)   ISBN 0 431 13930 X (paperback)
06 05 04 03 02   06 05 04 03 02
10 9 8 7 6 5 4 3 2   10 9 8 7 6 5 4 3 2 1

British Library Cataloguing in Publication Data
Spilsbury, Louise
    What does it mean to have sickle-cell anaemia?
    1. Sickle cell anaemia – Juvenile literature
    I. Title II. Sickle cell anaemia
    616.1'527

Acknowledgements
The publishers would like to thank the following for permission to reproduce photographs: Allsport USA/Zoran Milich, p.5; Image Bank/Ross Whitaker, p.14; Science Photo Library/Eye of Science, p.4; Stone/Andrea Booker, p.25, /Dave Nagel, p.23, /Rick Rusing, p.27, /Chad Slattery, p.22.

The following pictures were taken on commission for Heinemann: Trevor Clifford, pp.8, 9, 15–19, 24, 26; Maggie Milner, pp.12, 13, 20, 21, 28, 29.

The pictures on the following pages were posed by models who do not have Sickle Cell Anaemia: 5, 14, 15, 19, 23, 25, 27.

Special thanks to: Marsha, Darius, Rikki, Rami, Carlene, Edward, Steve and Rochelle.

The publishers would also like to thank The Sickle Cell Society; Dr P.J. Darbyshire, Consultant Paediatric Haematologist at Birmingham Children's Hospital for his help and comments; Julie Johnson, PHSE Consultant Trainer and Writer.

Cover photograph reproduced with permission of Trevor Clifford.

Contents

Any words appearing in the text in bold, **like this**, are explained in the Glossary.

What is sickle-cell anaemia?

Sickle-cell anaemia is a **disease** that affects the blood. Blood does a vital job in your body. It travels through the **blood vessels** (tubes) carrying food and **oxygen** to all parts of your body and collecting waste. **Red blood cells** are one of the main substances in your blood. Normal red blood cells are round and squashy – they look a bit like doughnuts. People with sickle-cell anaemia have some red blood cells that have become hard and curved like a new moon. This is also the shape of an old-fashioned farm tool called a sickle. That is why it is called 'sickle-cell anaemia'. It is one of several conditions called sickle-cell disease.

Because of their shape, sickle cells do not live as long as normal red blood cells. They do not move as freely through the blood vessels and can cause blockages when they get stuck. This causes people with sickle-cell anaemia to have problems such as tiredness, pain and swelling in different parts of the body. It also makes them more likely to suffer from **infections**.

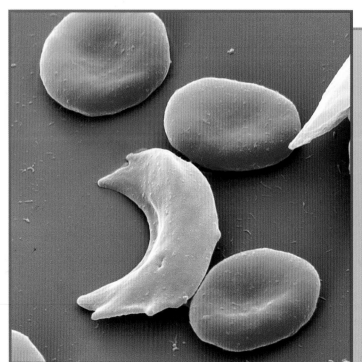

This picture shows you what normal (round) and sickle-shaped blood cells look like. They have been magnified (enlarged) 7,400 times so you can see them. Usually, one drop of blood contains about 1000 million red blood cells!

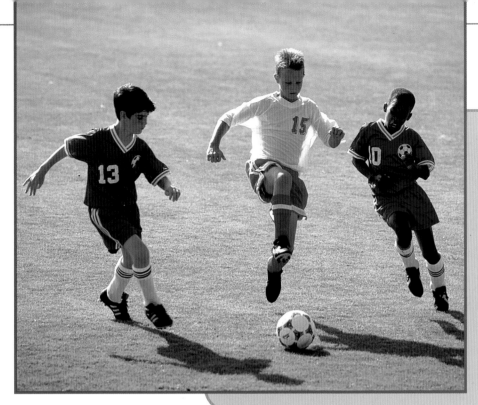

Young people with sickle-cell anaemia may have difficult or painful times, but most of them have the disease under control so they can get on with doing the things they enjoy.

How does it affect people?

Sickle-cell anaemia affects people in different ways. Some people hardly know they have it. Perhaps they have only one or two spells of mild pain in a year. Other people may have stronger pains more frequently, and they may have to miss school while they recover. With the right help and medicines, though, most people with sickle-cell anaemia feel fine for most of the time.

Who does it affect?

People who have sickle-cell anaemia are mainly from families whose ancestors came from Africa, the Caribbean, the Eastern Mediterranean, the Middle East and Asia. In Britain, most people who have sickle-cell anaemia are of African or Caribbean descent. This means that although they were born and grew up in Britain, their parents, grandparents or great-grandparents were born in Africa or a Caribbean country such as Jamaica, and moved to Britain to live.

What does blood do?

When you breathe, air comes into your body through your nose and your mouth. It then travels to your lungs. Your heart is a special muscle that pumps blood round your body all the time. Blood travels around the body in tubes called **blood vessels**. As blood passes through the vessels in the lungs, the **red blood cells** pick up **oxygen** from the air in your lungs. They carry it to all the other parts of your body as they move around with the blood.

Why do you need oxygen?

Your body is made up of millions of tiny living **cells**. These cells need energy for everything they do – to live, grow and repair themselves. Your body makes the energy it needs by mixing **chemicals** from food and oxygen together inside the cells. Your blood carries the chemicals and oxygen to the cells in your body.

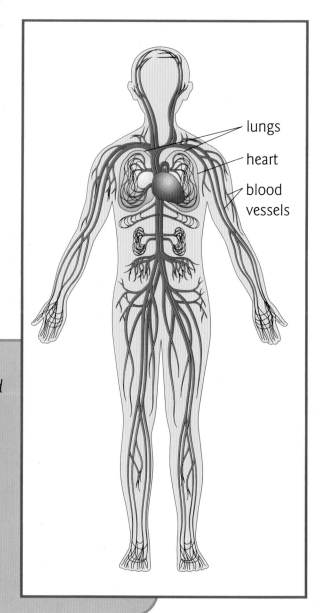

lungs

heart

blood vessels

One set of blood vessels (shown in red) carry red blood cells full of oxygen from the lungs. They travel around the body, releasing oxygen where it is needed. Another set of vessels (shown in blue) carry the blood cells back to the lungs to pick up more oxygen.

Changing shape

The main substance in all red blood cells is called **haemoglobin**. Haemoglobin is a bit like a bus on a road, carrying oxygen around the body through the blood vessels and dropping it off where it is needed. In people with sickle-cell anaemia, when the oxygen is released from the haemoglobin, the red blood cells become hard and pointed (sickle-shaped). Sickle-shaped cells cannot carry oxygen very well.

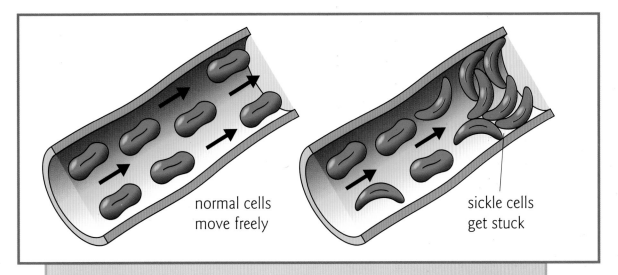

normal cells
move freely

sickle cells
get stuck

Because of their shape, sickle cells sometimes get stuck in smaller blood vessels and stop the blood flowing normally. This is what causes pain. Because blood travels all around the body, this can happen almost anywhere.

Normal red blood cells are soft and round so they can squeeze through tiny blood vessels. Sickle-shaped red blood cells have trouble passing through the body's smaller blood vessels. When some get stuck, they form a plug and stop blood reaching that particular part of the body. This is a bit like a traffic jam on a motorway. Normal red blood cells cannot get through and the oxygen they carry cannot reach that part of the body either. These blockages can be quite painful.

Problems of sickle-cell anaemia

Everyone is different and people with sickle-cell anaemia may have different problems at different times. The three main problems are pain, **anaemia** and **infections**. What causes them and what exactly are they?

Pain

When sickle-shaped **red blood cells** become stuck in a **blood vessel**, the **oxygen** supply to that part of the body is cut off. If the area is without oxygen for a long time, it can become damaged. In most cases the area just becomes swollen and sore, but it can hurt badly. This painful blockage of blood vessels is known as a '**crisis**'.

The blockages can happen almost anywhere, but they usually cause pain in the arms, legs, back and stomach. For some people the pain can be simply a bit annoying and may last only a few hours. For other people it can hurt a lot and it may last for several days. Sickle-cell anaemia can also make people's hands and feet swell up and their joints (the place where two bones meet, like your knees) ache.

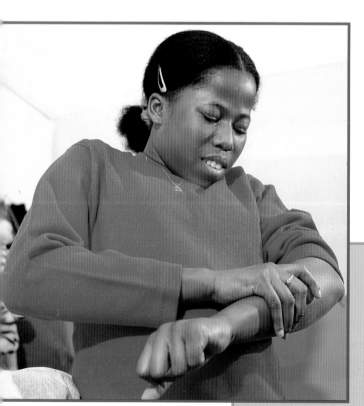

Young people with sickle-cell anaemia may get pain while they are at school. It is difficult to concentrate on work when you are in pain, and this means they may have to miss some school.

Just because you have sickle-cell anaemia does not mean you feel poorly all the time. Many people with sickle-cell anaemia feel perfectly fine most of the time.

Anaemia

A person with anaemia has too few red blood cells. Normal red blood cells live for 120 days before they are destroyed and the body makes new ones. Sickle cells last only between ten and twenty days. The body cannot make new red blood cells fast enough to keep up with this rapid loss. People with sickle-cells end up with fewer red blood cells than other people. This is called being anaemic. People who have anaemia look pale and may have times when they feel weak, tired or out of breath.

Infections

The spleen is a body part located behind your stomach. It is part of the body's immune system. Your immune system protects your body from infection by fighting the bugs that cause **disease**. When sickle cells cause repeated blockages to the spleen, it may become damaged. Children with sickle-cell anaemia are more likely to catch **infectious diseases**, because their body is unable to defend itself in the usual way. They may have to take medicine every day to help prevent infection.

Who gets sickle-cell anaemia?

People **inherit** sickle-cell anaemia from their parents. This means they are born with it, just as they are born with other family likenesses. The instructions for building your body are passed from parent to child in **genes**. There are genes for your height, hair colour, shape, and even the type of blood you have. Everyone has two copies of the **haemoglobin** gene – one from their mother and one from their father. The type of haemoglobin your parents have decides the type of haemoglobin you have.

If both parents have sickle-cell anaemia, their children will all have sickle-cell anaemia as well. However, if one parent has sickle-cell anaemia and the other does not, then all of their children will be born with sickle-cell trait. If you have sickle-cell trait it means you do not have sickle-cell anaemia and you are perfectly healthy, but you could pass the gene for sickle-cell anaemia on to your children.

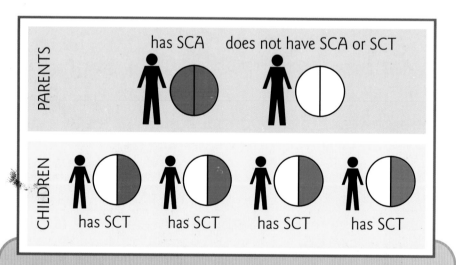

All the children in this family were born with sickle-cell trait (SCT). They do not have sickle-cell anaemia (SCA), but they could pass it on to their own children when they grow up if their partner also has sickle-cell trait.

If both parents have sickle-cell trait (SCT), there is a one in four chance that each child they have will be born with sickle-cell anaemia (SCA). All their children have a one in two chance of having sickle-cell trait. There is also a one in four chance that each child will be free of any sickle-cell problems.

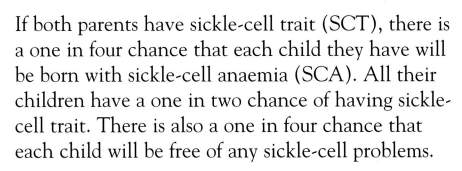

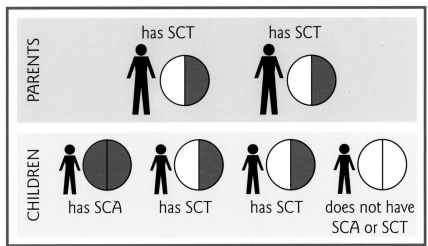

If one parent has sickle-cell trait (SCT) and the other has sickle-cell anaemia (SCA), each child that they have will either have sickle-cell trait or sickle-cell anaemia. None of this couple's children will be completely unaffected.

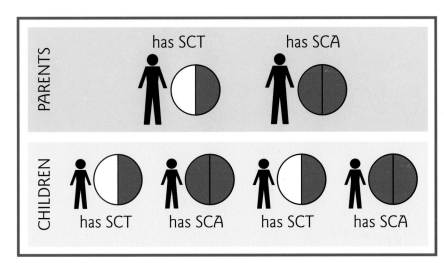

Chance
However many children a couple has, the 'chances' are the same for each new baby. For example, every baby a woman has could be a boy or girl. Even if she already has four boys, the chances of the fifth being a girl are still one in two.

Meet Maureen and Rikki

Hello. I'm Maureen, and I'm Rikki's mum. Rikki is eight now. We were told Rikki had sickle-cell anaemia when he was a baby. At the time I didn't really know what sickle-cell anaemia was. Luckily, the people at the hospital gave me good support and helped me understand what it is and what Rikki needs.

Doctors started him on **penicillin** medicine straightaway to help protect his body from **infection**. He had his first **crisis** at four months old, then again at one year old. He had a lot of pain in his legs and had to go to hospital. He still has two or three crises a year, but most of the time he feels okay. He still has penicillin every day and **folic acid** as well. This helps him make new **red blood cells**. He goes to the hospital regularly so the doctors can check how he is.

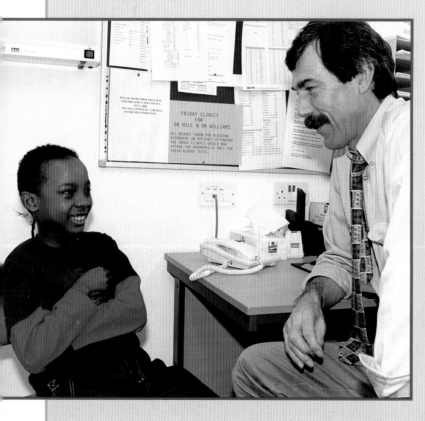

Most of the time Rikki just gets on with things, although he sometimes misses the odd day of school because he gets very tired. When this happens, he is really sensible and goes to bed early for a few days until he feels less tired.

I'm Rikki. I have to take medicines for my sickle-cell anaemia. I take them in the morning before school and in the evenings. I have them on a spoon or by **injection**.

Sickle-cell anaemia doesn't stop me doing things that I like. I just get tired sometimes. When that happens I listen to some music and that helps me relax, or I go to bed early. I really like reading. I read a lot of books. I do a lot of drawing at home, too. My little sister is called Angela and she likes me to do drawings for her. The other thing I like doing is playing board games – Monopoly is my favourite.

I like school. At school my best subjects are art and science. I sometimes play football with my friends at breaktime. But I don't like being cold and I have to be careful not to get too cold. When it's very cold outside I stay inside the warm classroom at breaktime and read a book or draw instead.

This is me and my mum. We read or draw while we are waiting at the hospital.

Tests and treatment

Most people with sickle-cell anaemia have good health most of the time. They may need to have medicines or other treatment only if the **disease** causes them bad pain or affects a part of their body in another way. Children are at greatest risk when they are very young. Between birth and the age of five, a small number of children have even died from **infections** or other problems brought on by sickle-cell anaemia.

Fortunately, doctors can tell if a baby has sickle-cell anaemia by doing a simple **blood test**. Then the baby or child must visit their doctor or hospital regularly. They also take **penicillin**, a kind of medicine that helps prevent them catching infections. It is very important to take the penicillin every day.

Testing for sickle-cell anaemia

To test for sickle-cell anaemia a doctor takes a pinprick of blood from the baby's heel, where they hardly feel it. In a laboratory a tiny electrical charge is passed through the **haemoglobin** to make it move. Haemoglobin with sickle-cell anaemia is easy to spot because it moves differently from other haemoglobin.

Most babies with sickle-cell anaemia get all the help they need to stay healthy and happy.

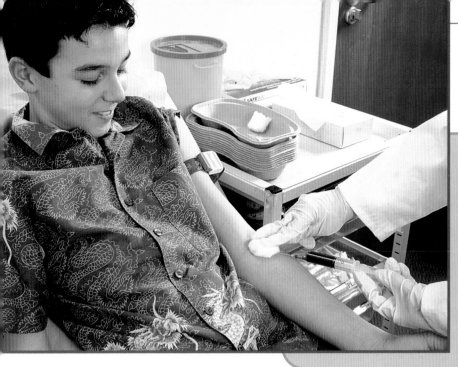

Blood tests are an important part of regular check-ups for people with sickle-cell anaemia.

Taking care of yourself

Young people with sickle-cell anaemia can do a lot to help themselves. One of the most important things they must do is visit their doctor or hospital clinic regularly. At these appointments the doctor examines them and they may have blood tests. This helps doctors spot any changes in their health so that these can be treated straightaway. It is also a chance for people to ask questions and to talk about how they have been feeling.

By taking care of themselves, people with sickle-cell anaemia can also protect themselves against infections and reduce the amount of pain they feel. We should all look after our bodies in order to keep healthy. We should all eat the right foods, including lots of fruit and vegetables, drink plenty of water, take lots of exercise and keep ourselves clean. People with sickle-cell anaemia also need to avoid getting very cold and make sure they have some extra time to rest. Being cold or overtired can bring on a **crisis**. Doing the right things helps people with sickle-cell anaemia lead a normal life.

When it hurts

People with sickle-cell anaemia find that different things can bring on **crises** (periods of pain). **Infections**, thirst, over-excitement, cold weather or even having an accident, like falling over, are all things that can trigger (start) a crisis. Many people can tell beforehand that they are about to have a crisis. Some people feel thirsty, or they may feel cross or more tired than usual.

Jaundice

Some people get jaundice before a spell of pain. Jaundice makes people's skin and the whites of their eyes look a bit yellow. Jaundice can be caused by **anaemia**. The jaundice itself is not a problem. The yellowy look of the skin goes when people are better. However, jaundice is sometimes a sign that a spell of sickle-cell pain is coming.

Some people keep a diary to help them work out if something in particular causes their pain. Sometimes crises just happen. Don't worry, there are lots of things you can do to help you get on with your life.

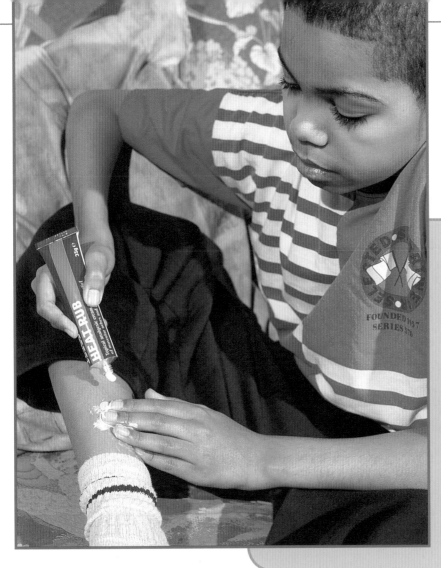

Some people find that rubbing cream on the sore part of their body helps to ease the pain. The warmth and movement help to get the blood flowing in that area again.

Ways to help

Lots of crises happen with no obvious cause. Then there is nothing for it but to find ways of making yourself feel more comfortable and easing the pain. There are many things you can do to stop or ease your pain. Some people find that putting their feet up and having a rest is enough to make them feel better. Other people hold something warm, like a hot water bottle, on the affected area to help soothe the pain. If these measures do not work, or if the pain is very strong, people may need to take **painkillers**. Painkillers are a kind of medicine that you can take to stop you feeling a pain. Some people take them if they get a headache, for example. You usually take them in tablet form.

Controlling anaemia and infections

Children with sickle-cell anaemia tend to have a lower number of **red blood cells** in their body than other people. This is called being anaemic. They may feel quite well most of the time, but if the **anaemia** gets worse they are left feeling tired and poorly. As the problem is a low red blood cell count, they need help increasing the number of red blood cells that they make.

Folic acid is a kind of **vitamin**, found in many of the fruits and vegetables that we eat. Folic acid helps our bodies make new blood cells to replace the old ones, which are always wearing out and being replaced. Many people with sickle-cell anaemia take folic acid tablets regularly. This helps them keep their number of red blood cells up, and the problems of anaemia down.

Eating fruit and vegetables helps to keep us all healthy. As well as taking folic acid tablets, people with sickle-cell anaemia can help themselves feel better by eating a healthy diet.

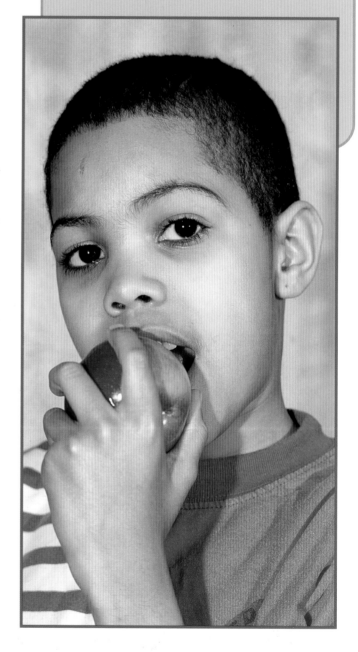

Tackling infections

Many people with sickle-cell anaemia find that they are more likely to catch **infections** than other people. They also have a harder time fighting them off once they have them. They may need to take **penicillin** every day. This medicine works to prevent infections. It is also important for children with sickle-cell anaemia to have vaccinations. Vaccinations are **injections** of vaccines, which help our bodies fight off infections. People with sickle-cell anaemia have the same vaccinations as everyone else. They may also have extra ones, including one to stop them catching influenza ('flu).

How do vaccines work?

Vaccines are made from dead or damaged germs (tiny living things that cause **disease** when they are alive). In vaccinations doctors or nurses inject a safe amount of the germ that causes a particular disease into your body. This helps your body make **antibodies** to fight the disease. These allow your body to destroy that disease if you should ever come across it later.

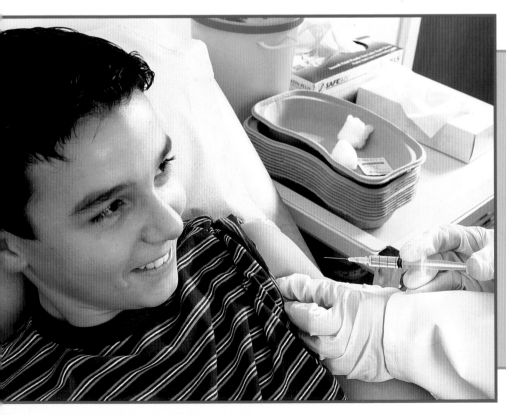

Lots of people don't like the idea of vaccination injections, but they don't really hurt and they help your body protect you from disease.

Meet Carlene

I'm Carlene and I'm thirteen years old. Mum and dad found out I had sickle-cell anaemia when I was born, after the doctors did a **blood test**. When you tell people, it seems like this major thing, but it's really just a small part of my life. I've got it all under control. My mum doesn't really need to do anything much – I deal with my medicines myself.

Four nights a week I have to have medicine through a needle and it goes in overnight. There's a little pump that keeps the medicine going in even while I'm asleep. First I have to clean the bit of my leg or stomach where I'm going to put the needle. Then I put on a bit of cream to make it numb (so I won't feel the needle going in). It doesn't hurt a bit. Then when I've put the needle in and attached the pump I can do whatever I like. I usually just sit and watch TV until bedtime, but the pump is so small you can walk about with it alright.

Once a month I have to go to hospital for a blood transfusion. This means that doctors give me a fresh lot of healthy blood to stop the effects of the sickle-cell anaemia. The transfusion is usually on a Monday and I have to visit the hospital on the Thursday before for cross-matching. That's a kind of check that doctors do to make sure that they have got the right sort of blood ready for me on the Monday. Most children with sickle-cell don't need this type of treatment.

I have to miss a day of school when I go on a Monday. But the people at my clinic are really nice and I don't mind going at all. I don't get behind with schoolwork because I take homework with me to do while I'm waiting at the hospital. There are even teachers there to help you with schoolwork. They have helped me catch up with some subjects that I missed on Mondays, especially with maths because at one time I was getting behind on that. I'm good at most subjects, except maths!

Living with sickle-cell anaemia

Everyone has different experiences of living with sickle-cell anaemia. For some children, the **disease** hardly affects their day-to-day life at all. For others, it may be something that they have to be aware of all the time. Most people realize that if they are sensible and have a positive outlook they can keep sickle-cell anaemia from interfering too much with their everyday life. This may mean always remembering to do certain things, such as drinking plenty of water because being **dehydrated** can bring on a **crisis**, and they need to wrap up warm on chilly days.

Join a club!

Many families who have children with sickle-cell anaemia like to join support groups. These are groups of people who have experience of the same disease. It can help to talk to someone who understands. It can also help to know that you are not alone – that there are other people who are going through the same kind of things as you. Lots of sickle-cell anaemia groups organize day trips and special outings for their members. They meet to share stories and ideas, as well as to have fun.

Some people say that having sickle-cell anaemia has made them more determined to make the most of their lives.

How does it feel?

Many children who have sickle-cell anaemia feel angry sometimes. They feel that it is unfair that they should have a disease when other people, including perhaps their brothers and sisters, do not. If they have bad pains often, they may get fed up with being in and out of hospital or feeling poorly. Being in pain can make you feel miserable. At times like this you will need your friends and family.

Yet, in spite of the bad times they sometimes have, most young people with sickle-cell anaemia don't feel sorry for themselves and don't want other people to feel sorry for them. They say that even though their life is interrupted by a painful crisis from time to time, they mostly just get on with their lives, just like anyone else. Some say that having sickle-cell anaemia has made them more careful about taking care of their body and taking responsibility for themselves. Many children find that this makes them more capable and independent than other people their age.

At school

Sickle-cell anaemia does not affect how clever you are. It has nothing to do with your intelligence or your ability to get on with other people. Most children with sickle-cell anaemia go to ordinary schools and join in with all the usual activities, just like everyone else. There are just a few things that their teachers and classmates need to know.

Children with sickle-cell anaemia may need to store medicines at school, such as **painkillers**, so they can take them if they have any pain during the day. They also need to be able to have a drink of water or juice, even during lesson time, because being **dehydrated** can bring on a painful **crisis**. That also means they need to go to the bathroom more often, and it may be easier for them if they don't always have to ask.

Children with sickle-cell anaemia can sometimes get tired. It is useful if the school knows this in case they need to rest. This gives them the chance to recover so they can work or play as well as other people.

Sports day

Some people are better at some kinds of sport than others. On sports day, a child with sickle-cell anaemia who is a good runner is just as likely to win a race as anyone else. However, if you have sickle-cell anaemia you may sometimes feel breathless and short of energy. Sickle-shaped **red blood cells** cannot carry **oxygen** very well, so people with sickle-cell anaemia sometimes feel out of breath. You may find that you are better at sports like basketball or volleyball, where you don't need to run for long distances.

People with sickle-cell anaemia may also be better with indoor sports because it is easier to keep warm. Cold, damp weather can bring on a crisis for some people. Swimming is fine indoors at a heated swimming pool where there are warm changing rooms.

We all like some sports better than others. Children with sickle-cell anaemia can do as much exercise as they feel happy doing. If you keep fit you are less likely to have a crisis.

At home

Most of the time, home life for people with sickle-cell anaemia is the same as it is for anyone else. Home is somewhere we can relax and do the things that we enjoy.

Sometimes, however, children with sickle-cell anaemia end up missing school and spending more time at home than other children. If they have periods of pain, they may need to stay at home to rest and recover. Now, it might sound great to have some time off school, but it can be boring if it happens a lot and you are stuck in bed all the time. That is why it can help to be prepared. Most children with sickle-cell anaemia make sure that they have a good supply of books, videos, puzzles and games at home. Some children, if they feel up to it, may try to keep up with their schoolwork while they are at home.

We all have times when we have to stay in bed or at home because we are ill. It is much easier to cope if you can lose yourself in a good book or find something interesting to make or do.

Getting away

Sickle-cell anaemia is unpredictable. A **crisis** can happen any time, anywhere. At least at home and school people with sickle-cell anaemia can keep it pretty much under control because they know what is happening from day to day. Yet what happens when they go away on holiday or a school trip?

This should not be a problem. Everyone should make a checklist when they go away, to make sure they don't forget anything they need. For children with sickle-cell anaemia it is just the same – except that any medicines they need, such as **penicillin** or **painkillers**, should be top of the list. If the trip is abroad and they plan to fly, they should let the airline know they have sickle-cell anaemia. They will need to drink during the flight and get up and move around sometimes. Otherwise they need holidays for the same reason as everyone – to get away from it all, relax and have fun!

On holiday or out on a trip people have got more exciting things to do than worry about their sickle-cell anaemia.

Meet Barbara and Rochelle

Hello. My name is Barbara and my daughter is called Rochelle. She is eight years old. We found out that Rochelle had sickle-cell anaemia when she was a very young baby. Doctors took a blood sample from her heel and did a **blood test**. Then, on her first birthday she had a very serious **crisis**. She was very poorly for a while and we were very worried about her, but the hospital soon made her comfortable and she has not had a serious crisis since then.

Now we have the sickle-cell anaemia under control. Rochelle visits the hospital every six months so her doctor can check she is well and growing properly. She takes **penicillin** and **folic acid** every morning before school. This helps to keep her well. The only other thing she has to be aware of is keeping warm, especially after swimming lessons when it's important that she gets warmed up quickly. You should never let yourself get cold if you have sickle-cell anaemia. Apart from that, sickle-cell anaemia does not stop Rochelle from doing anything.

Hi. I'm Rochelle. I have to take medicine every day for my sickle-cell anaemia. I have a drink of orange juice afterwards because I don't like the taste of it. Sometimes I forget to take my medicine, but my mum reminds me. She is a school nurse so she checks I am well. She's always telling me to keep myself warm and putting hats and scarves on me. I get fed up with having sickle-cell anaemia sometimes because I can't wear short tops in case I get too cold. If I get very cold it's hard for me to get warm again.

I like doing lots of different things. I like skipping, chess and dominoes. I play chess with my granddad and aunty. I like riding my bike in the park at the back of our house. At school I like playing hide and seek and dominoes with my friends. I think my worst subject is English and my best subject is painting and drawing.

Glossary

anaemia disease which people can get when there are not enough red cells (and therefore haemoglobin) in their blood. People with anaemia are pale and tired because their body is not getting enough oxygen.

antibodies part of your body's defence, or immune system. When germs enter your body, blood cells make antibodies, which attach themselves to the germs and destroy them.

blood test when doctors take a tiny amount of blood and test it to find out if someone is well, or not

blood vessels tubes through which blood travels around the body

cells tiny living building blocks that make up all the parts of your body and of all living things. You can see cells only with a powerful microscope.

chemicals great variety of substances that can do many different things. Some chemicals in the brain help to transmit messages from one nerve cell to another.

crisis when sickle cells block a blood vessel causing pain

dehydrated when your body is short of fluid and you feel very thirsty

disease when part of a person's body is not working properly and they become ill

folic acid kind of vitamin that helps the body make new blood cells

genes substances within the mother and father that determine what their baby is like

haemoglobin main substance in red blood cells. It is red and gives blood its colour. It carries oxygen around the body.

infection when a germ gets into the body it causes an infection. If an infection makes you ill it is called an infectious disease.

infectious diseases when an infection makes you ill, you are said to have an infectious disease, such as influenza ('flu) and measles.

inherit when something is passed from parents to their young. Inherited diseases are hard to cure, but treatment can lessen most harmful effects.

injections one way of taking medicine. This is usually done with a fine needle, which is inserted under the skin, so that the medicine is then absorbed into the blood.

oxygen gas that is in the air all around us. Red blood cells take oxygen to the cells in your body, where they mix with food to give you energy.

painkillers range of medicines that ease pain, such as back pain or headaches

penicillin medicine that can help treat some infections. It can be taken in tablets or injections.

red blood cells the cells that give blood its red colour. They contain the substance called haemoglobin, which takes in oxygen in the lungs.

vitamin nutrient found in some of the foods we eat. Nutrients help us to grow and keep well.

Helpful books and addresses

BOOKS
Sickle-cell Anaemia, George Beshore, Franklin Watts, 1994

Sickle Cell Disease, Dr Ian Franklin, Faber, 1990

Sickle Cell – Did You Know? Sickle Cell Society, 2001
Available from the Sickle Cell Society or via e-mail:
sicklecellinfo.line@btinternet.com

Your Body: Blood, Anna Sandeman, Franklin Watts, 1996

Body Systems: Blood and Circulation, Jackie Hardie, Heinemann Library, 1996

ORGANIZATIONS AND WEBSITES
Sickle Cell Society
54 Station Road
London NW10 4UA
Telephone: 020 8961 7795/4006
Fax: 020 8961 8346
E-mail: sicklecellsoc@btinternet.com
The Sickle Cell Society offers counselling and support to those with sickle-cell disorders and their families.

IN AUSTRALIA
Australian Department of Health and Aged Care
Central Office
GPO Box 9848
Canberra ACT 2601
Telephone: (02) 6289 1555
Freecall: 1800 020 103
Fax: (02) 6281 6946

Index